108 Quotes

on Meditation

Amma

108 Quotes on Meditation

Published by:

> Mata Amritanandamayi Center
> P.O. Box 613
> San Ramon, CA 94583-0613, USA

In India:

> www.amritapuri.org
> inform@amritapuri.org

In USA:

> www.amma.org

In Europe:

> www.amma-europe.org

1.

Meditation is as valuable as gold. It leads to material prosperity, peace and liberation. Even a moment spent in meditation is never a waste. It can only be of great value.

2.

In addition to our meditation practice, if we also have compassion, then it is like gold with a wonderful fragrance! Meditation enables us to fill our heart with compassion.

3.

Making the mind one-pointed is the essence of all spiritual disciplines. One of the best methods for this is meditation.

4.

My children, when you sit for meditation, do not think that you can still your mind immediately. At first, you should relax all parts of your body. Loosen your clothes if they are too tight. Make sure the spine is erect. Then close your eyes and focus on your breath.

5.

You can start to meditate by focusing on the form of your Beloved Deity or the formless, for example, the light of a candle. If the mind wanders, bring it back. If you are unable to do that, then it is enough to watch where the mind is going. The mind should be kept under observation. Then it will stop running around and come under your control.

6.

Sit and gaze at the form of your Beloved Deity for two minutes. Then, close your eyes and visualize that Deity's form in your heart. Meditate by focusing the mind either on the spot between the eyebrows or in the heart. Whenever the form fades away, gaze again at the picture. Even though the picture is made of paper and ink, imagine that it is filled with consciousness. We can attain the Real only through the unreal. Because we are immersed in the unreal, we forget the Real. Through a picture we can be reminded of the Real.

7.

Initially, you will have to strive hard to focus on your Beloved Deity in meditation. In the beginning it may not be possible to visualize the full form. Even then, do not get depressed but continue trying to visualize only the feet of the Deity. In due course, you will be able to visualize the full form. Through the power of persistent practice, the form will become clearer and clearer.

8.

In the initial stages, ten minutes to half an hour of meditation twice a day is enough. Gradually, the duration can be increased. The time from 5 p.m. to 11 a.m. is good for meditation. You should sit silently for some time after meditating. Only then will you get the full benefit of your meditation. Always seek the advice of your spiritual teacher and strictly follow his or her instructions.

9.

While meditating, don't place the mind in any kind of tension. If any part of your body is tense or feels any pain, the mind will linger on that. Relax every part of the body and watch your thoughts with absolute awareness. Then the mind will subside by itself.

10.

Once you start getting a taste for meditation, sitting will not be difficult. It will slowly become spontaneous. Until then you must strive hard, otherwise it is difficult to teach patience to the body and mind.

11.

We shouldn't sit for meditation immediately after eating. After a heavy meal, a minimum of two hours should elapse before we sit for meditation. An interval of half an hour will be sufficient if we have eaten only a light snack.

12.

Can you sit and meditate in an untidy, dirty, ugly place? No, you can't. You need a clean and orderly place for that. If the place is dirty and untidy, it will affect your mind so that you won't be able to concentrate.

13.

You don't have to believe in God in order to meditate. You can imagine yourself merging with the Infinite just as a river merges with the ocean. This method will certainly help one to escape from feeling agitated.

14.

My children, meditation is not just about sitting with our eyes closed. We should make every action a form of worship. We should be able to experience God's presence everywhere.

15.

Once you have surrendered yourself fully and your whole being is in a state of constant prayer, what then remains is not you, but God. All that remains is love. Prayer can achieve this miracle. Your tears can accomplish this feat. What is the purpose of meditation? To become love, to experience that Oneness. The best meditation technique is to pray and to cry for God.

16.

Meditating doesn't just mean sitting in a lotus posture with your eyes closed. Meditation also means to selflessly serve people who are suffering, to console those who are in distress, to smile at someone and to say a few loving words.

17.

My children, don't try to still your mind by force when you sit for meditation. If you do that, the thoughts will rise up with ten times their original power. Try to find out from where the thoughts arise, and control them with that knowledge.

18.

By changing a common misconception—that our problems are in the outer situations of life—we can remove our problems once and for all. Understand that the difficulties are within your own mind. Once you become aware of this, you can begin the process of removing your inner weaknesses. Meditation is the method that is used to achieve this. Only the inner silence, stillness, and relaxation that we gain through meditation will help.

19.

Meditation is the technique that allows you to shut the doors and windows of the senses, so that you can look within and see your True Self.

20.

When we meditate on God with form, we are also meditating on our own Self. With all other thoughts restrained, our mind can become concentrated on the image of God. Eventually, there will be no thoughts except that of God.

21.

Meditation dissolves the fear of death. It makes us egoless and takes us to the state of no-mind. Once we transcend the mind, we realize that we are the unchanging, imperishable Atman (the Supreme Self), which is the essence of the universe.

22.

Any spiritual practice you do benefits the entire world. The vibrations from your japa (repeating a mantra), chanting and meditation, purify the atmosphere as well as your own mind. Without even being aware of it, you spread peace and quietude to those who come in contact with you.

23.

Although our true nature is that of the ever-free, eternal Atman, at present our understanding is that we are bound and limited. To remove this misconception, spiritual practices like meditation are necessary.

24.

Through spiritual practices such as meditation, we gain power. We become a storehouse of inexhaustible energy and vigor. We become capable of performing righteous actions without breaking down in trying situations.

25.

You are not going to reach God without patience and attention. How will you get concentration when you meditate if you can't be alert when it comes to even small things on the gross plane? Meditation is extremely subtle. It is the attention and patience we show in the little things that leads us to great achievements.

26.

Either proceed according to God's will, convinced that "Everything is You," or inquire "Who am I?" with the strong conviction that "Everything is within me."

27.

When there is seva (selfless work) to do, spiritual aspirants should forget themselves and become completely immersed in that work as an offering at the Lord's Lotus Feet. At the same time, if there is no work, then the same person should be able to sit in meditation for long hours.

28.

Our mind becomes impure by the many different thoughts that constantly arise. Meditation directs all those thoughts toward one point of focus.

29.

Children, the mind is naturally one-pointed and pure, but up until now we have made room for many impure worldly emotions that are like bad tenants. We have given them a small piece of our land on which to build a hut. Now they pay no attention when we ask them to leave; instead they rush forward to pick a fight with us. We have to work hard to kick them out or take them to court. Likewise, to kick out the tenants of the mind, we have to file a case in God's court. It is a constant fight. We must continue fighting until we become victorious.

30.

Duality exists only when we are identified with the body. Once this identification is transcended, all dualities disappear. In that state of Supreme Oneness, it is like a vessel has broken open, and the space inside the vessel becomes one with the totality of space.

31.

Ten hours of meditation in the daytime is equal to five hours of meditation at night. Even if you sleep the whole day, you will not get the same freshness and happiness you will get from a few hours of sleep at night. This is because the atmosphere is calm and quiet at night. There are fewer worldly vibrations and thoughts, making the atmosphere conducive to meditation. In the daytime, the atmosphere is completely polluted with the worldly thoughts of people running after material pleasures.

32.

Only a selfless attitude supported by prayer, meditation and mantra chanting can restore the lost harmony of the human mind. First, harmonize the mind. Then the harmony of Nature will spontaneously take place. Where there is concentration, there is harmony.

33.

Through meditation, mental agitation is overcome. Meditation helps us to purify the mind the way a filter removes impurities from water. When the mind then becomes absorbed in something, we experience our innate joy.

34.

Meditation is beneficial even for small children. Their intelligence will become clear, their memory enhanced, and it will be easy for them to learn. They will then become strong in body and mind and will be able to face life boldly.

35.

Concentration and love are one. They are inseparable, like the two sides of a coin. You have to feel love if you want to experience concentration in meditation because it's impossible to separate them.

36.

Genuine meditation is the end of all misery. All suffering is caused by the mind, and the past is of the mind. Only by letting go of the past, which can be achieved through meditation, is it possible to become established in the Self or God.

37.

We should meditate regularly and sincerely, without stopping, until we attain one-pointedness of mind. Once the seeds are sown, we should water them every day until the seedlings grow and reach a certain level. It may take some time for the sprouts of spirituality to emerge. Sprinkle the waters of spiritual practice regularly without fail and wait patiently.

38.

As you meditate more, you will experience that more vasanas (latent tendencies and desires) will come up. It is only for the purpose of being destroyed that the vasanas arise in this way.

39.

To make the mind meditate by force is like pushing a hollow log of wood under water. It will shoot up to the surface as soon as you remove your hand. We should slowly try to conquer the mind by giving it new ideas and cultivating good habits in the place of old, bad habits.

40.

We should watch our thoughts from a distance. If we go near them, they will drag us along without our knowledge, but if we watch from a distance, we can see the thoughts settling and peace returning.

41.

Before meditating, you should tell your mind, "Whatever may happen, I will get up from here only after the predetermined time of meditation is over."

42.

Though we initially see God in a particular Deity and call God by a particular name, when our devotion matures and blossoms fully, we will come to see God in all names and forms, and within ourselves.

43.

If you speak just after meditating, all the energy you have gained will be wasted. Don't waste your energy like a person squandering his hard-earned wealth on mere peanuts.

44.

Darling children, always remember in your heart that God is Love. By meditating on the embodiment of Love, you yourselves will become this Love.

45.

Love should be born within. Through meditation, prayer and chanting, we can nurture and nourish this love, creating a conducive atmosphere where love can grow.

46.

Meditation is the technique of knowing how to be in the present moment. It is an experience. It cannot be explained verbally. Meditation happens when you go beyond your mind and all your thoughts.

47.

We should be able to transmit the inner silence and stillness we gain through our meditation, into our actions. In fact, meditation helps us to gain a deeper insight into all aspects of our life.

48.

A river that flows through many branches will not have a powerful current. If the branches are redirected and the river is made to flow only through one main stream, the force of the current will increase greatly. Similarly, at present our mind flows out toward hundreds of sense objects. If the mind is controlled and focused on one point, tremendous power will be generated, which can be used to do wonderful things.

49.

Meditation helps us to see everything as a delightful play so that even the moment of death becomes a blissful experience.

50.

My children, in our present state of mind, our so-called "selfless actions" are not always completely selfless. We should therefore try to keep a perfect balance between actions and meditation. Introspection, contemplation, prayer and chanting are necessary in the beginning stages of spiritual life. As we grow in our attitude of selflessness, our meditation will grow deeper and deeper.

51.

Crying for God for five minutes is equal to one hour of meditation.

52.

Negative thoughts may arise during meditation. If this happens, you should think, "O mind, is there any benefit in cherishing such thoughts? Do they have any value?" You should think in this way and thereby reject unnecessary thoughts.

53.

Without love, no amount of mantra repetition or meditation will bear fruit. When your love for God becomes extraordinarily strong, all the negative tendencies within you will automatically drop away. Rowing a boat against the current is difficult, but if the boat has a sail, it becomes easy. Love for God is like a sail that helps the boat move forward.

54.

To remember God, you have to forget. To genuinely be focused on God is to be fully and absolutely in the present moment, forgetting the past and the future. That alone is true prayer. This sort of forgetfulness will help you to slow down the mind and experience the bliss of meditation.

55.

In meditation you become silent, and remain at rest in your own True Self.

56.

You will recognize someone who meditates by his or her character. The meditator will be humble and will have the attitude that "I am nothing." Only if we develop an attitude that "I am the servant of everyone," is God's vision possible.

57.

Smiling is one of the highest forms of meditation.

58.

You can change or transform your fate
through the self-effort of meditation and
sincere prayer.

59.

Only actions performed with an attitude of selflessness can help you to go deeper into meditation. Genuine meditation will take place only when you have become truly selfless, because it is selflessness that removes thoughts and takes you deep into silence.

60.

The art of relaxation in meditation brings out the power that exists within you. It is the art of making your mind still and focusing all your energy on the work you are doing. Thus, you will be able to bring out all of your full potential. Once you learn this art, everything happens spontaneously and effortlessly.

61.

Even when you meditate on the name or form of a God, Goddess or Amma, you are, in fact, meditating on your own Self—not on some external object.

62.

As your concentration increases, your thoughts decrease. When the thoughts decrease, your mind and intellect will become subtler, allowing for deeper meditation.

63.

Meditation and other spiritual practices give us the power and courage to smile at death.

64.

Remember God, chant God's name, meditate on God's form and repeat your mantra. This is the best medicine to heal the wounds of the past. Take this medicine to let go of the past, and do not be anxious about the future.

65.

Meditate with the conviction that your Beloved Deity resides in your own heart.

66.

My children, never fail to practice your daily routine. No matter how tired or sick you are, you should try to sit and meditate for some time.

67.

In the beginning, you need to develop a feeling of love for your daily meditation routine. It should become an essential part of your life. If you cannot do your spiritual practice at the set time, you should feel the pain of having missed it and the longing to do it.

68.

If you can see with a subtle eye, you will find that there's a gap between thoughts. This gap is thinner than a hair's breadth, but it's there. If you can keep the thoughts from flowing without control, as they do now, this gap will increase. This is possible only in a meditative mind that concentrates on a single thought. In meditation, the mind must dwell on one single thought, not on many thoughts.

69.

When you have finished sitting in meditation, do not immediately get up and engage in other activities. After releasing your legs from the meditative posture, lie in savasana (the corpse posture) for five to seven minutes. Relax both the mind and body. Allow sufficient time for the flow of prana (vital energy) to return to its normal state. It is during this time that the positive effects of meditation are fully assimilated by the body.

70.

Group meditation is very beneficial. The atmosphere becomes permeated with the vibrations of everyone's concentration, which makes it more conducive for meditation. Since everyone's thought vibrations are of a similar pattern at this time, good concentration can be attained.

71.

The mind is nothing but thoughts. Thoughts, when intense, become actions. Actions, when repeated, become habits. Habits form our character. To still the mind in meditation, we first have to change the quality of our thoughts.

72.

A health tonic has a certain prescribed dosage beyond which it can be quite harmful. If you gulp down the whole bottle of tonic, it will only cause you harm. Similarly, when doing spiritual practices like meditation, you may be very enthusiastic about it, and you may think, "Let me meditate for hours together." If you are not ready, this can lead to many problems. Your head can become heated; you may not get proper sleep; your digestion can be affected, etc. Approach meditation in a very progressive way—slowly and steadily.

73.

It is the nature of the mind to wander. It cannot be quiet. When we try to quiet the mind by concentrating on an object of meditation, we can see that it wanders even more. Beginners may feel frightened or discouraged by all those countless thoughts. Constant practice coupled with determination is the only way to conquer the mind. Don't feel frightened or discouraged. Continue your spiritual practice with determination.

74.

My children, during meditation, negative thoughts may arise in the mind. Don't worry. Don't pay any attention to those thoughts. Giving negativity too much importance will weaken the mind. The mind is just a collection of thoughts. Think that the bad thoughts come up because it's time for them to disappear. Be careful not to identify with them. Just ignore any negative thoughts and continue your meditation.

75.

In the beginning stages of meditation, the latent tamas (sluggishness) will surface, making one feel sleepy. This should be overcome by regular, systematic practice, control of food, etc. When you feel sleepy, immediately get up from your meditation seat and chant your mantra while walking back and forth. Use a mala (rosary) while chanting, holding it close to your chest with alertness. If one is vigilant, these tamasic qualities will vanish in due course. Let rajas (activity) drive away tamas.

76.

When thoughts pass through your mind during meditation, watch them but do not relate to them. Don't cling to them. As the thoughts pass through your mind, try to develop the ability to stand back as a witness. This will make your mind strong.

77.

Do your meditation and spiritual practices to the best of your ability and don't think about the result. If you sit thinking about the result, you won't be able to do the practice with full attention. A spiritual aspirant is not supposed to care about obtaining spiritual experiences. Run straight toward the goal!

78.

Genuine prayer IS meditation. It is communion with God that takes place in the quiet stillness of our heart.

79.

At some stage, the spiritual aspirant merges with the Beloved Deity. We will merge with the Divine through the intense love brought about by the constant remembrance of the Deity, and the renunciation of every other thought. Our Beloved Deity will then lead us to the final state of the non-dual experience, where all that remains is pure awareness, joy and bliss.

80.

Only a person who lives a moment-to-moment life can be completely free from fear. That person alone will be able to embrace death peacefully. This moment-to-moment living is possible only through meditation and other spiritual practices.

81.

All spiritual practices are done in order to be content in one's own Self, by the Self, and for the Self. We should become independent—depending only on our own Self, the very source of all joy.

82.

In order to feel completely relaxed and to finally reach the state of Perfect Aloneness, the interference of the past and the future has to cease. Only this moment exists and should be experienced.

83.

Meditation will help us to gain control over our mind and our body. It will enable us to develop patience. The remote control of the mind should be in our hands. At present, it is not like that. We are under the control of our senses.

84.

Authentic meditation can only be experienced in the presence of a Satguru (True Guru). Such a Guru is constantly in a state of meditation, even though you may see him or her being physically active. The Guru's presence is the most conducive place for your Self-unfolding to take place. In the Guru's presence you can attain that inner aloneness, and thereby let go of all your fears and feelings of otherness.

85.

When, through meditation, the little ego disappears, we become the Limitless and Impersonal and can experience the Ocean of Bliss. The remains of what appears to be the ego will be there, but it is not real.

86.

When we are meditating or sitting alone, we may feel that there are no negativities within us. Still, when we find ourselves in daunting situations, all the negativity arises and becomes difficult to control. Running away from situations will never help us. Wherever you are, use that situation to gain control over your mind. That is really the aim of spiritual practices.

87.

God will be the servant of the person who has gained one-pointedness of mind in meditation. My children, Amma can guarantee this. Just try, and see what happens!

88.

Those who pray to God and meditate on God sincerely will not experience a shortage of anything essential.

89.

Effort is human, while grace is divine. Effort is limited; grace is unlimited. Your limited human effort can take you only to a certain point. From there, the Guru's grace will carry you to the goal. Do your spiritual practice sincerely with an attitude of self-surrender and love, and then patiently wait for the grace to come.

90.

Because you haven't created the clouds in the external sky, they won't disappear as a result of your observing them. However, the clouds of thought in the inner sky will dissolve if you can simply witness them.

91.

Both movement and stillness are two different aspects of the same truth. They are one. To reach the state of stillness, it is necessary to hold onto something.

92.

In the olden days, Amma would not sit idle even for a moment. She would always meditate. If someone would come to talk, Amma would see them as the form of Devi. They could talk as much as they liked. If one moment was lost, Amma would feel terrible distress, thinking, "O God, this much time was wasted." Then she would do twice as much spiritual practice. You will also get the fruit if you try with such urgency.

93.

The whole purpose of meditation is to become nothing—to let go of the attitude of doership. Even the feeling, "I am meditating," is incorrect. In real meditation there is no "I." When the attitude of "I" and "mine" has vanished, we will be of service to everyone and no longer be a burden to others. An ordinary person can be compared to a small, stagnant pond, while Self-realized souls are like a river or a tree, giving comfort and coolness to those who come to them.

94.

If you are unable to meditate, try to repeat your mantra. If you also find that to be difficult, then sing the Divine Names. In whatever way, we must strive hard to attain the constant remembrance of the Supreme. Do not let the mind think unnecessary things.

95.

Humility will come as one progresses in meditation. Humility means seeing God in everything or perceiving one's own Self everywhere. Humility means self-surrender—surrendering our will to the will of God. In this state, there are no more reactions, only acceptance. Then we feel love toward all creatures. We are able to see everything as God.

96.

It is good to meditate in dim light. External light can be a disturbance when we are trying to illuminate our interior.

97.

Spiritual practices such as meditation, repetition of a mantra and singing bhajans, are different methods to relax the mind so that you can always be open, like a freshly blossomed flower.

98.

In order to steady your mind and make it still, you need to be attached to something higher than the mind. The mind is the noisiest place in the world. Unless there is some divine form on which it can contemplate or meditate, the mind will not be quiet. However, the object of one's meditation or contemplation should not be anything familiar, for then the mind will soon get bored.

99.

As you drink in the object of your meditation, you become one with it. In that kind of participation, you are totally absent. It is as if the player is absent—only the play exists. The singer is absent—only the song exists.

100.

One who really loves is constantly in a meditative mood. Thoughts cease to exist in the presence of such love. The true lover only meditates. All their thoughts are about the Beloved, so there are not numerous thought waves in their mind. Only one thought prevails, and that singular thought is about the Beloved.

101.

When there is only one thought, there is no mind. The lover's constant single-minded focus on the Beloved touches the innermost recesses of the heart, where words and speech cannot reach. The devotee gets drawn into a constant state of meditation. At that point, the two become one.

102.

Meditation prevails in real love. You become silent and remain at rest in your own True Self. One cannot speak when one becomes at rest in one's own Self.

103.

Don't overstrain yourself to try to sit in lotus posture or hold your breath to meditate on the Deity's form. Meditation is remembrance of God, constant and loving remembrance. Consider the Deity as your most loved one, as your parent, or just consider yourself as their child. Remember your Beloved Deity whenever you can, no matter where you are or what you are doing. Strive to feel the Deity in your heart. Endeavor to feel their divine presence, grace, compassion and love.

104.

Pray until your heart melts and flows down as tears. It is said that the water of the Ganges River purifies whoever takes a dip in it. The tears that fill the eyes while one is remembering God have tremendous power to purify one's mind. These tears are more powerful than meditation. Such tears are verily the Ganges.

105.

The best way to get concentration is by crying to the Lord, and that, in fact, is meditation. This is what great devotees like the gopis and Mirabai did. See how selflessly Mirabai prayed, "Lord, it does not matter if You don't love me. But, O Lord, please do not take away my right to love You." They prayed and cried until their whole being transformed into a state of constant prayer. They kept on worshipping the Lord until they were totally consumed by the flames of Divine Love. They themselves became the offering.

106.

Meditate, pray and chant your mantra to remove your anger and its cause. As far as a spiritual aspirant is concerned, removing anger and other negative tendencies is life's goal. They dedicate their entire life to that.

107.

The food of worldly thoughts and desires is harmful. There is food far tastier and healthier: our spiritual practices. Once you experience this, start to feed the mind regularly with meditation, chanting the divine name, japa and other spiritual practices. Slowly the hunger to have more and more of this spiritual food will grow.

108.

If you are concerned about the welfare of the world, then you should sincerely meditate and do spiritual practices. My children, become like the lighthouse guiding the ships sailing in the dark. Shine the light of God in the world!